The Nature and Science of
ENERGY

Jane Burton and Kim Taylor

Gareth Stevens Publishing
MILWAUKEE

For a free color catalog describing Gareth Stevens Publishing's list of high-quality books and multimedia programs, call 1-800-542-2595 (USA) or 1-800-461-9120 (Canada). Gareth Stevens Publishing's Fax: (414) 225-0377. See our catalog, too, on the World Wide Web: http://gsinc.com

Library of Congress Cataloging-in-Publication Data

Burton, Jane.
The nature and science of energy / by Jane Burton and Kim Taylor.
p. cm. -- (Exploring the science of nature)
Includes index.
Summary: Describes different kinds of energy and explores some properties of energy and some of the different forms that it can take.
ISBN 0-8368-1941-1 (lib. bdg.)
1. Force and energy--Juvenile literature. [1. Force and energy.] I. Taylor, Kim. II. Title.
III. Series: Burton, Jane. Exploring the science of nature.
QC73.4.B87   1998
530--dc21   97-34235

First published in North America in 1998 by
Gareth Stevens Publishing
1555 North RiverCenter Drive, Suite 201
Milwaukee, Wisconsin 53212 USA

This U.S. edition © 1998 by Gareth Stevens, Inc. Created with original © 1998 by White Cottage Children's Books. Text and photographs © 1998 by Jane Burton and Kim Taylor. The photographs on pages 7, 9 (below), 15, 16 (right), and 27 are by Mark Taylor. Conceived, designed and produced by White Cottage Children's Books, 29 Lancaster Park, Richmond, Surrey TW10 6AB, England. Additional end matter © 1998 by Gareth Stevens, Inc.

The rights of Jane Burton and Kim Taylor to be identified as the authors of this work have been asserted by them in accordance with the Copyright, Design and Patents Act 1988. Educational consultant, Jane Weaver; scientific adviser, Dr. Jan Taylor.

Printed in the United States of America

1 2 3 4 5 6 7 8 9 02 01 00 99 98

Contents

Words that appear in the glossary are printed in **boldface** type the first time they occur in the text.

Natural Energy

Energy in nature comes in many different forms. Heat is a form of energy. It comes mainly from the Sun. In smaller amounts, it comes from other things, such as forest fires and our bodies. Light is another form of energy. It comes from the Sun and stars. Some animals and even plants also produce small amounts of light energy. Radio waves and **ultraviolet** rays are other forms of energy. Electricity is a form of energy, as well.

All these different forms of energy can be changed, one into another. For instance, the electrical energy in lightning is gone in a flash. It instantly changes into brilliant light, heat, and sound, which is heard as thunder.

Most of Earth's energy — wind, waves, heat, and light — comes from the Sun. The Sun itself is powered by **nuclear energy**.

Top: Every animal, even a small snail, uses energy to move.

Opposite: When lightning flashes, electrical energy stored in clouds changes into light, heat, and sound energy.

Left: The Sun is the main source of energy for Earth. Its light allows many living things to see. Its warmth creates wind and draws water into the air to form clouds.

Energy Waves

Top: A raindrop falls in a pond, causing ripples that spread out in **concentric** rings.

Energy travels through space like waves moving across the surface of water. Heat, light, and other types of radiant energy travel in the form of **electromagnetic waves**. The distance between waves — called **wavelength** — determines the type of energy. For instance, radio waves may be several feet (meters) apart. The measurement between the waves of radiant heat and between the waves of light is much smaller.

Right: A mute swan treads water and beats its wings, causing waves to spread out. These are like the energy waves that spread out from the Sun.

Electromagnetic waves travel through space in straight lines at the vast speed of about 186,000 miles (300,000 kilometers) per second. So, even the longest waves, radio waves, arrive at Earth at an incredibly high rate. This is called the **frequency** of the radio signal, and it is another way of looking at wavelength. If you were at the beach and counted how many waves crashed on shore every minute, you would know the frequency of the waves. The frequency of light waves is much greater than that of radio waves. Many billions of light waves reach your eyes every second!

Above: A massive wave, carrying a huge amount of energy, breaks against the rocks.

Kinetic Energy

Energy cannot be destroyed, but it can be changed from one form into another. When a cat climbs a tree, it uses energy to make its way to the top. When the cat is high above the ground, its body has what is known as **potential energy**. When the cat leaps from the tree, the potential energy is converted into **kinetic energy** — the energy of movement. The noise that is heard if the cat lands on a tin roof is some of the kinetic energy converted into sound energy.

Top: A yellow-necked mouse leaps vertically into the air. Its kinetic energy will become potential energy when the mouse reaches the top of its jump.

Right: When a cat leaps, its body gains kinetic energy.

Left: In the late afternoon in Botswana, storm clouds gather. The water they contain represents potential energy. This energy will be released when rain falls to the ground.

Below: Water high in the mountains has potential energy. This energy is released as the water comes rushing down in rivers and crashing over waterfalls.

Clouds store huge amounts of potential energy because of all the water they hold high above the ground. This potential energy began as heat from the Sun. The Sun caused evaporation of water from the sea, resulting in the formation of clouds. Potential energy in clouds is converted into kinetic energy when rain falls. Some of the energy may be converted into electricity during thunderstorms. Rain falling on mountains retains some of its potential energy that can then be used as water to power **hydroelectric** generators.

Noisy Energy

Top: Some birds, such as this rook, use energy to produce a loud cry.

Opposite: Sound waves are reflected like other types of energy waves. This bat listens to the echoes of its own high-pitched squeaks and uses the information to navigate.

Sound travels in waves, but the waves are not electromagnetic. Instead, sound waves are **compression** waves. These are waves of slightly compressed air that travel at about 1,115 feet (340 m) per second. Sound has to travel through a **medium** — air, water, wood, or some other substance. It cannot travel in outer space or through a vacuum because there is no air there that can be compressed.

To produce sound, an object has to vibrate. For example, a plucked guitar string vibrates, causing compression waves to travel outward from it. The energy that made the string vibrate converts into sound.

Sound is very important to many animals. They communicate with each other through sound waves. The calls of whales travel over 60 miles (100 km) in the sea.

Right: A cricket sends a shrill song into the Australian night by rubbing its wings together.

10

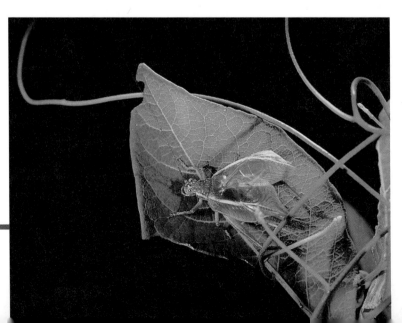

Energy Does Work

When a squirrel eats a nut, the energy stored in the nut is used by the squirrel to do work. The work a squirrel does might include running along the branch of a tree. The squirrel's muscles convert energy from the nut into kinetic energy. But there is another sort of work that the nut's energy can do — it keeps the squirrel warm.

If there is work to be done, there must be energy to do it. Mammals and birds are **warm-blooded**, and many are very active. They need a constant supply of energy to keep them on the move. **Cold-blooded** animals, such as fish, use much less energy. Fish, for instance, glide through water much more easily than mammals move on land. Surprisingly, it takes hardly any energy at all to keep a streamlined fish moving at a steady speed. It will continue gliding forward for some time after it has actually stopped swimming. Energy is required to get the fish moving again and speed it on its way. It is this acceleration that requires energy, not simply movement on its own.

Opposite: Leaping from a stream to catch a passing fly is work for the brown trout. It needs energy to accomplish this task.

Top: A baby Siberian chipmunk eats a grape that will give the chipmunk energy for its muscles to work.

Below: The nut this gray squirrel is eating will provide it with energy to scamper around and keep warm.

Storing Energy

Top: Sweet chestnuts burst forth each autumn, packed with energy.

Energy is not always easy to store. Light cannot be placed in a bottle and kept there. Even heat is difficult to store. You can put hot water in a bottle, but the heat does not last. The only type of energy that can be stored for any length of time is **chemical energy**. Chemical energy has been stored underground in the form of coal and oil for millions of years.

Plants have developed many different ways of storing chemical energy. A nut is a concentrated energy store. It contains carbohydrates and oil,

Right: The baobab or boab tree stores energy in its bulbous trunk.

14

both of which are rich in energy. It is no wonder squirrels enjoy nuts! Of course, the energy in nuts is not intended to be only fuel for squirrels. Hopefully, some of the nuts grow into new trees.

Some plants, such as potatoes and carrots, store energy in their roots. Onions store energy in their leaf bases. Sago palms and baobabs store energy in their stalks.

Above: Energy stored in the roots of the yellow skunk cabbage grows this magnificent flower in spring. The energy also produces enough heat for the flower to melt its way up through the snows of winter.

Right: The barking gecko lives in Western Australia, where temperatures are warm most of the year. The gecko stores energy in its tail in the form of fat.

Most animals store chemical energy in their bodies in the form of fat and oil. Fat and oil contain more energy than other organic materials. Many animals store fat in a layer just under the skin. Fat is a good **insulator** to protect animals against the cold. Species that live in hot climates, however, do not need to be insulated. They store fat in other ways. For instance, camels have fatty humps on their backs, and geckos and some sheep have thick, fatty tails.

Right: Pikas are related to rabbits and hares. They cut and dry grasses and other plants in the Sun to make hay. They store the hay to eat during winter months when food is scarce.

Before fat can be converted into usable energy, it has to be chemically changed so that it can be carried by the animal's blood to its liver. There, the energy is stored temporarily in a form that is ready for immediate use.

Some animals not only store energy inside their bodies, but also collect stores outside their bodies. Mice, squirrels, beavers, and several bird species spend busy days during autumn gathering nuts, seeds, and other foods to provide them with energy over the winter months.

Saving Energy

Top: The African white butterfly flies when the Sun shines. But it dives into a bush when a cloud appears. Here, it rests with its wings closed to save energy.

Energy is vitally important to humans and other animals. Sometimes energy is in short supply, so it makes sense to save it whenever possible. Sleeping in a warm bed with plenty of covers is one way of saving energy. A lion with a full stomach may sleep for two days. During this time, the lion does not need to hunt.

Some birds are expert at saving energy. Vultures glide for hours without flapping their wings. They do this by circling in air currents that keep them aloft. Birds called shearwaters and albatrosses spend nearly all their time over the sea far from shore. They are masters of the air, gliding effortlessly just above the surface of the water. They make use of air currents generated as the wind sweeps over the waves.

Right: White-backed vultures save energy by soaring upward on a rising air current.

Many mammals save energy during winter by **hibernating**. They go into a state of inactivity for several months, and their bodies become cold. Small bats that sleep during the day and hummingbirds that sleep during the night save energy while they sleep by letting their bodies become cold.

Above: A common dormouse saves energy by hibernating during winter. Its body temperature drops, and its breathing becomes slow and shallow.

Energy from the Sun

The Sun is the source of almost all the energy that is used by plants and animals on Earth. Without the Sun's rays, there would be no life. But animals cannot use sunshine directly, except to warm their bodies. They have to absorb chemical energy from their food. Plants, on the other hand, possess the secret of converting the Sun's rays into chemical energy.

Sunlight — not heat — is used by plants to make food. Most plants are green but, surprisingly, green is the one color that is not used by plants. Leaves look green because they reflect green light. Other colors in sunlight are absorbed and used in a complex process whereby **carbon dioxide** from the air and water in the leaves are converted into oxygen and sugar. This process is called **photosynthesis**. The sugar contains energy from sunlight converted into a chemical form.

20

Burning Energy

Top: The coal tit burns up a great deal of energy in its daily activities.

Making sugar with energy from sunlight is just the first stage in plant growth. Many of the sugar **molecules** join together in long strings to form **cellulose**. Cellulose is a tough carbohydrate. It is the material that makes plants strong. It forms the basis of wood, which is further strengthened by a substance called **lignin**. As many as three thousand sugar molecules link to form a single cellulose molecule.

Cellulose contains energy. When a wooden log is burned, the energy in it is released as heat. Burning combines oxygen from the air with the **carbon** and **hydrogen** of cellulose and lignin, and produces carbon dioxide and water vapor. This is just the reverse of photosynthesis except that most of the energy given out is heat, whereas the energy taken in during photosynthesis is light.

Below: A puppy springs into a leap.

He comes down with paws out, ready for a landing.

Left: Energy from the Sun that was used to make these twigs and branches is released as heat when the wood burns.

Mammals and birds burn carbohydrates to keep themselves warm. Carbohydrates and oxygen combine in their muscles to produce carbon dioxide and water, and to release energy in the form of muscle movement and heat. There are no flames, of course, because this chemical burning takes place at a very low temperature.

As his front paws touch down, his hind legs swing forward...

ready to push him onward again. All this action burns up a large amount of energy.

Borrowing Energy

Green plants use sunlight for energy. But not all plants are green. **Fungi** are many different colors except green. They rely on green plants to collect the energy they need. Most fungi grow on dead plant material that still contains some of the energy trapped when the plants were alive. Some fungi also grow on living plants.

Animals cannot use the Sun's energy to make food. They have to rely on the energy stored in plants. **Herbivores** eat leaves that have trapped the Sun's rays and stored the energy in chemical form. Even **carnivores** rely on plant energy since they, in turn, eat herbivores.

Right: This blue wildebeest looks up with a mouthful of succulent grass. The magnificent animal gets energy from grass that has absorbed the Sun's energy.

Left: Leopards get energy from red meat. They hunt plant-eating animals. So this energy is third hand — having passed from the Sun to green plants, and then to herbivores.

Below: The flowers of many Australian trees produce so much nectar that some birds and bats live on it exclusively. This red wattlebird drinks nectar from an acorn banksia flower.

Many flowers produce a very powerful energy source called nectar. Bees collect it to make honey, and many other insects and birds feed on it. Nectar is so rich in energy that insects can spend large amounts of energy collecting it. Many nectar-feeders use some of the energy from the nectar to keep their wing muscles warm so they can fly quickly from one flower to the next. The muscles of all animals work better when they are warm. Even on a cold day, a nectar-gathering bee's muscles are at around 98.6° Fahrenheit (37° Centigrade) — the same as a human's. Hawkmoths, which hover as they feed on flowers, can raise their muscle temperature to 115° F (46° C) — positively hot! This allows them to dart around in search of energy-rich nectar.

The Greenhouse Effect

For millions of years, energy has been pouring down onto Earth's surface from the Sun — and energy is indestructible. So where has all this energy gone? Some of it has been trapped by plants and borrowed from them by animals. But this is only a tiny fraction of all the energy that reaches Earth from the Sun. Most of the Sun's energy is radiated back into space.

Earth is surrounded by **atmosphere** that acts like a blanket to keep most of Earth's surface at a livable temperature. If Earth had no atmosphere, heat from the Sun would quickly radiate back into space. That would mean our days would be baking hot and our nights would be freezing cold.

The efficiency of the atmosphere depends on the gases it contains. The most important of these gases are carbon dioxide and water vapor. These allow radiant heat in from the Sun, but keep it from leaving again, in much the same way that glass traps heat in a greenhouse. Coal and oil burning in power stations and gasoline burning in cars add vast amounts of carbon dioxide to the atmosphere, making Earth warmer. This is called the **greenhouse effect**.

Above: On a clear night in the North American desert, Joshua trees withstand bitter cold. Earth would be much colder — and the trees would not survive — without the blanket of carbon dioxide and other gases in the atmosphere.

Activities:

Energy Is Everywhere

The fact that energy constantly changes from one form to another makes it seem like it is a quick-change artist. Just when you think you know what energy is, suddenly it changes into a totally different form. But two things are certain — energy never disappears, and it never appears from out of nowhere.

Scientists once thought that energy and matter (the material of the Universe) were two completely different things. Then they discovered that energy and matter are interchangeable. Tiny amounts of matter convert into huge amounts of nuclear energy. The Sun produces nuclear energy from hydrogen gas. Day by day, the Sun's mass decreases, as matter is converted to energy.

Below: Potential energy stored in the twisted rubber band is converted into kinetic energy as the "mouse" creeps forward.

The Clockwork Mouse

If a certain amount of energy is put into a system, the same amount of energy can be retrieved from it — although what comes out may be in a different form.

To create a simple energy system, try making this clockwork mouse. You will need an empty thread spool, a standard-sized candle, two wooden matchsticks, a nail file, glue, and a tough rubber band slightly longer than the spool.

Have an adult cut a section of candle about 1/2 inch (1 centimeter) long. Then have the adult carefully bore a hole through the candle section's middle with a nail file. Scrape a matchstick-sized groove across one end of the candle section. Now thread the rubber band through the candle section and through the spool, securing the ends with matchsticks (*see photo*). The matchstick that rests against the spool should be broken off so that it is shorter than the diameter of the spool. Secure the matchstick with glue after passing it through the rubber band. The other matchstick should rest in the groove of the candle section so that one end projects well beyond the edge of the spool. This is your mouse.

Put some energy into your "mouse" by holding the spool and winding the matchstick around 20-30 times. A twisted rubber band stores potential energy. Place the mouse on the floor and watch it creep forward. The potential energy in the rubber band converts into kinetic energy. The candle section acts as a brake, slowing the rate at which energy from the band is released. If you have a cat, it will watch the "mouse" with fascination.

Mud Craters

This experiment needs to be done outdoors while you are wearing old clothes. You are likely to get spattered with mud.

The most important thing you need is the right kind of mud. It has to be thick and creamy like whipped cream, but not liquid. The best places to find mud are on muddy riverbanks and mud flats near the sea, or in muddy areas that were once puddles that are drying up.

Above: The size of the craters made by a large and a small pebble, dropped together, show how much kinetic energy each was carrying. Potter's clay was used instead of mud in this experiment.

Next, find two smooth, round pebbles — one about 1/2 inch (1 cm) across and the other about 1 inch (3 cm) across.

Hold the pebbles, one in each hand, as high as you can above the mud. Then drop the two pebbles at the same time. Gravity causes the pebbles to accelerate while they travel downward. As they gather speed, their potential energy becomes kinetic energy until they hit the mud with a "splat."

The first question is, did the two pebbles hit the mud at the same moment? They should have. Even though gravity is pulling harder on the bigger pebble, more energy is needed to get the bigger one moving, so it accelerates at the same rate as the smaller one. When the pebbles hit the mud, the size of the crater each one makes shows how much energy each had.

Experiment further and give one of the pebbles some extra kinetic energy by throwing it toward the mud. Even a small pebble can carry a lot of energy if it is traveling fast enough.

The final question is, where has all the energy that was in the pebbles gone? Some of it became kinetic energy in little bits of mud flying out in all directions. Some of it became potential energy in the raised rim of the craters. But mostly it became heat — heat that you would not notice — because a lot of kinetic energy creates only a little heat. The mud around the craters became just a fraction of a degree warmer.

Below: This dog saves energy by soaking up warmth from the fire. The kittens receive energy from the dog by snuggling close to her.

29

Glossary

atmosphere: the layer of air and clouds that surrounds Earth.

carbon: an element that is found in all living things.

carbon dioxide: a gas made from carbon and oxygen.

carnivore: a living being that eats meat.

cellulose: a tough carbohydrate found in nearly all plants. Cotton and paper are made of cellulose fibers.

chemical energy: the energy used to make a chemical substance. The energy is released when the substance is broken down.

cold-blooded: an animal that has a body temperature that changes with the temperature of its environment.

compression: the squeezing of a substance into a smaller space.

concentric: having the same center.

electromagnetic wave: the form in which heat, light, and other types of energy travel through space.

frequency: the number of waves that arrive at a fixed point in a set period of time.

fungi: plants that have no flowers, leaves, or green coloring, such as mushrooms.

greenhouse effect: a warming due to the trapping of the Sun's radiation.

herbivore: an animal that eats only plants.

hibernating: slowing down body processes in winter to save energy.

hydroelectric: when water power is used to make electricity.

hydrogen: a gas; it is the simplest and lightest of the chemical elements.

insulator: material through which heat and electricity cannot easily travel.

kinetic energy: the energy that an object possesses by virtue of its movement.

lignin: a complex carbohydrate that is a major constituent of wood.

medium: a type of material. Gases, liquids, and solids are different kinds of media. Space is not a medium because it has no matter.

molecule: the smallest part of a substance, made up of two or more atoms that are joined together.

nuclear energy: energy that comes from the nuclei of atoms, such as the Sun's energy.

photosynthesis: a process in which plants use energy from the Sun to make food.

potential energy: the force an object possesses because of its position or condition. Potential energy is stored, waiting to be released.

ultraviolet: invisible radiation that has a wavelength shorter than that of violet light.

warm-blooded: an animal with a body temperature that stays about the same no matter what the temperature of the environment is.

wavelength: the distance between two similar points on successive waves.

Plants and Animals

The common names of plants and animals vary from language to language. But plants and animals also have scientific names, based on Greek or Latin words, that are the same the world over. Each plant and animal has two scientific names. The first name is called the genus. It starts with a capital letter. The second name is the species name. It starts with a small letter.

Books to Read

Alternative Energy (series). *Bioenergy. Geothermal Energy. Solar Energy. Water Energy. Wind Energy.* Graham Houghton & Graham Rickard (Gareth Stevens)

Earth Power. Madelaine Yates (Abingdon)

Energy. Irving Adler (Day)

Energy. Andrew Langley (Bookwright)

Energy. Illa Podendorf (Childrens Press)

Energy at Work. John Satchwell (Lothrop)

Energy: Simple Science Experiments for Young Scientists. Larry White (Millbrook Press)

The Science Book of Energy. Neil Ardley (Harcourt Brace Jovanovich)

Science Works! (series). *Energy.* Steve Parker (Gareth Stevens)

Videos and Web Sites

Videos

Energy. (New Dimensions Media)
Energy for the Future. (Encyclopædia Britannica Educational Corporation)
Energy: Less Is More. (Churchill Media)
The Energy Series. (Barr Films)
Energy Sources. (Barr Films)
Energy: What Is It? (United Learning)
Solar Energy. (Barr Films)

Web Sites

www.energy.ca.gov/education/
www.wam.umd.edu/~tfagan/enrgyenv.html
tqd.advanced.org/3684/
www.windows.umich.edu/photoscience.la.
   asu.edu/photosyn/study.html

Index